Prambanan Temple at Yogyakarta

INDONESIA

BY PATRICK RYAN

THE CHILD'S WORLD®

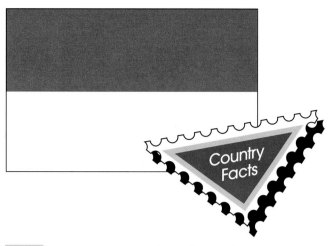

Country Facts

Area: 741,000 square miles. That is about three times the size of Texas.

Population: About 200 million people.

Capital City: Jakarta.

Other Important Cities: Surabaya, Bandung, Medan, and Semarang.

Money: The rupiah.

National Language: Bahasa Indonesia is the official language of Indonesia. Many people also speak English.

National Holiday: Independence Day, August 17.

National Flag: Indonesia's flag has two colors; red and white. The red stands for bravery. The white stands for purity and truth.

Head of Government: President General Soeharto.

Library of Congress Cataloging-in-Publication Data
Ryan, Pat (Patrick M.).
Indonesia / by Pat Ryan.
Series: "Faces and Places".
p. cm.
Includes index.
Summary: Provides basic information about the land, climate, history, and culture of Indonesia, the world's largest archipelego.
ISBN 1-56766-275-7 (library bound)

1. Indonesia — Juvenile literature. [1. Indonesia.] I. Title.
DS615.R93 1998   96-7524
959.8 — dc20   CIP
                                          AC

GRAPHIC DESIGN
Robert A. Honey, Seattle

PHOTO RESEARCH
James R. Rothaus / James R. Rothaus & Associates

ELECTRONIC PRE–PRESS PRODUCTION
Robert E. Bonaker / Graphic Design & Consulting Co.

PHOTOGRAPHY
All photography from Michele Burgess except:
cover: Balinese Girl by Dave Houser/Corbis;
page 8: Island of Java by Jack Fields/Corbis;
page 10 : Rafflesia Flower by Frank Lane Picture Agency/Corbis;
page 18: City Life in Jakarta by Dan Lamont/Corbis

Table of Contents

Where Is Indonesia?

If you could fly high up in the air, you would notice that Earth is made up of land areas surrounded by water. These land areas are called continents. If you could look more closely, you would see that some of the continents are actually made up of many different countries.

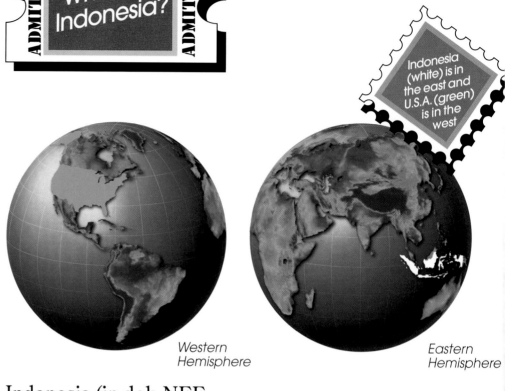

Western Hemisphere

Eastern Hemisphere

Indonesia (white) is in the east and U.S.A. (green) is in the west

Indonesia (in-doh-NEE-zhuh) is an island country located in Asia.

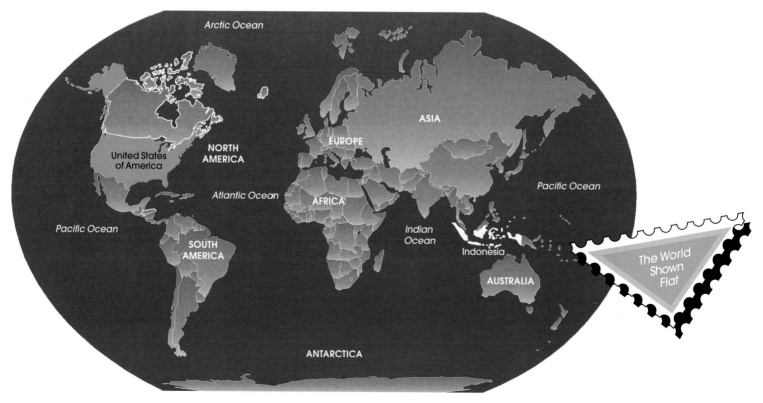

Arctic Ocean

ASIA

EUROPE

NORTH AMERICA

United States of America

Atlantic Ocean

AFRICA

Pacific Ocean

Pacific Ocean

SOUTH AMERICA

Indian Ocean

Indonesia

AUSTRALIA

The World Shown Flat

ANTARCTICA

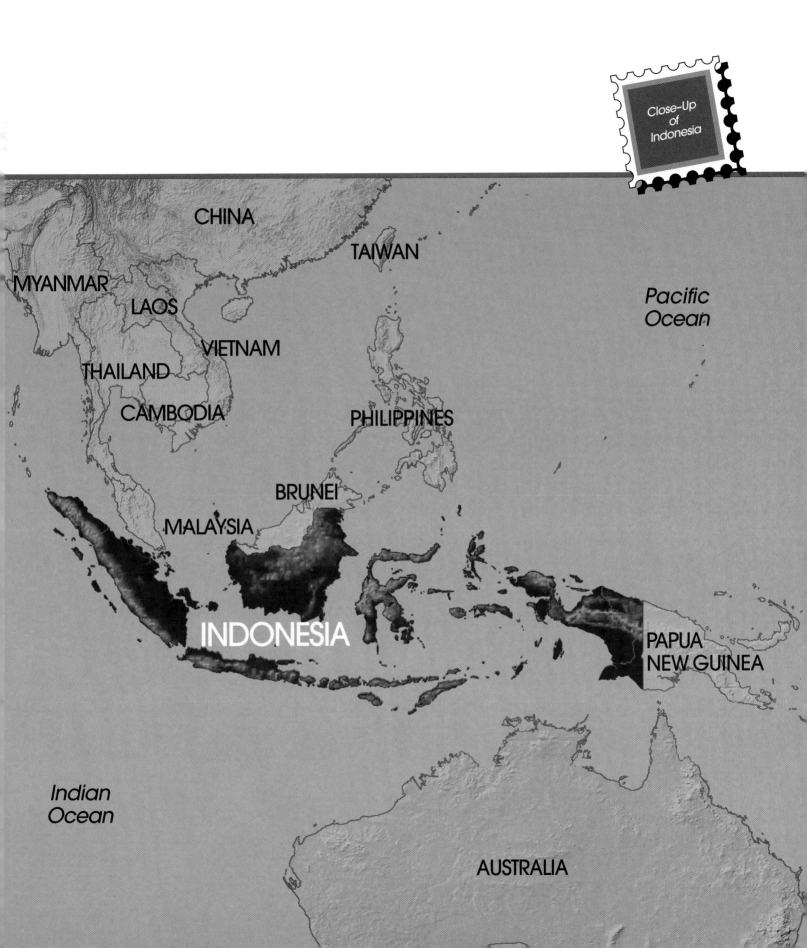

CHINA

TAIWAN

MYANMAR

*Pacific
Ocean*

LAOS

VIETNAM

THAILAND

CAMBODIA

PHILIPPINES

BRUNEI

MALAYSIA

INDONESIA

PAPUA
NEW GUINEA

*Indian
Ocean*

AUSTRALIA

SUMATRA

BORNEO

SULAWESI

NEW GUINEA

● Bamba Puang
Valley

JAVA
Yogyakarta ●

Evening
Moon
Over The
Island Of
Java

Bamba Puang Valley On Sulawesi

Instead of being one piece of land like most countries, Indonesia is made up of many small islands—more than 13,000! The islands stretch for almost 4,000 miles between the Indian and Pacific oceans. Many of Indonesia's islands are very tiny. Most of the islands don't even have people living on them. The five largest islands in Indonesia are New Guinea, Borneo, Sumatra, Java, and Sulawesi. Most of the people in Indonesia live on these islands.

Rain Forest Of Sumatra

Plants & Animals

Huge rain forests cover some of the islands in Indonesia. Here you can find the world's largest plant—the rafflesia (ruh-FLEE-shuh). This giant plant grows up to three feet wide and weighs twenty pounds!

Komodo Dragon

Rafflesia Flower

Many different kinds of animals live in Indonesia, too. Birds, monkeys, elephants, and rhinos all make their homes in the thick rain forests. Deer and wild pigs also live on Indonesia's islands. On one island there are even giant lizards called Komodo dragons. These huge creatures eat the deer and goats that live in the forests.

Sumatran Tiger

SUMATRA

*Rafflesia
Flowers*

*IRIAN
JAYA*

KOMODO

Crocodiles
Of
Irian Jaya

Borobudur Temple
On
Java

Borobudar • • Yogyakarta

Baliem
Valley

Long Ago

People have been living in Indonesia for a very long time. In fact, more than a million years ago, humans called Java people lived on the island of Java. Slowly, other people came to the island. Over time, these people formed little kingdoms. They moved and spread out to Indonesia's other islands. These kingdoms ruled Indonesia for hundreds of years.

Dani Tribesman Of Baliem Valley

Sultan's Palace In Yogyakarta

After the little kingdoms, Indonesia was ruled by people from other countries. These visitors thought Indonesia was the perfect stopping place for their ships. They made Indonesian obey new rules that they did not like.

Finally, after World War II, the people of Indonesia began to rule their own country. Today, Indonesia is a proud country with many proud people.

Roman Catholic Church In Jakarta

Man In Festival Dress Near Lake Toba

Unloading Timber In Sulawesi

Lake Toba

SULAWESI

Jakarta

BALI

Temple
Festival
On
Bali

TANA
TORAJA

BALI

SUMBA

Barong
Dancer
From
Bali

Man And Daughter From Sumba

About 200 million people live in Indonesia. Many belong to small groups called tribes. Each tribe has its own special ways and ideas. Each tribe also has its own language. Even though they may not always understand one another, Indonesians are happy and friendly people. Many like to dance and listen to music.

On some islands, men play in gamelan bands for fun. Gamelan music is made by striking flat bells called gongs. Some gamelan bands have more than fifty gongs!

At night, many people enjoy puppet plays. The puppets are all worked by one man called a dalang. Gamelan musicians play at the shows.

Gamelan Orchestra From Bali

Tambourine Player From Sulawesi

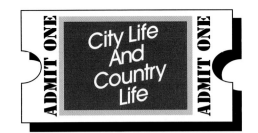

City Life In Jakarta

Jakarta is the capital city of Indonesia. A capital city is where the government of the country works. Jakarta is also one of the largest cities in the world. People who live in Jakarta and other cities usually live in crowded apartments or small houses. Sometimes whole families sleep in the same room! Most city people work in factories. They make clothes, shoes, electronic instruments, and video games.

Country people are very different from city people. In the country, people are used to the old ways of life. Many live in simple huts and villages. They hunt animals and gather nuts and berries for food. In Indonesia, sometimes the old ways of doing things are better than the newer ways.

Village House In Southern Sulawesi

Street Scene In Medan

Medan

SULAWESI

Jakarta

Maros

Maros Area With
Bugis
Houses

BORNEO

KALIMANTAN

SULAWESI

BALI

Bali Girl
Working
In Rice
Field

Since there are many different tribes and languages in Indonesia, teaching young children can be difficult. So until students reach the third grade, they are taught in the language of their tribes. Then they are taught the common language of Indonesia— Bahasa Indonesian. Many children in Indonesia leave school after the sixth grade and go to work in the fields. This way they can make money and help their families.

Muslim Schoolgirls In Southern Sulawesi

School In Kalimantan

Ikat Weaver From Sumba

Over half of the people in Indonesia are farmers. Many grow rice for their families. They also sell rice to other countries. While rice is nice, Indonesian farmers also grow and sell rubber, tobacco, sugar, coffee, and tea.

Boats With Logs On Mahakam River

Many people who do not work in the rice fields work in Indonesia's rain forests. Here they cut down trees to be used for furniture and paper. However, many forest workers are very careful not to cut down too many trees. If they did, it might endanger plants, animals, and even other people.

Mahakam
River

BALI

SUMBA

Rice
Harvesting
On Bali

Boy Cooking Satay On Borneo

Roadside Stand On Sulawesi

Indonesians eat many different kinds of foods. Soup, fruits, and vegetables are all favorite foods in Indonesia. And almost everyone likes to eat rice. Indonesians put many different types of things on top of their rice to make different dishes. Some put crab or spicy beef on top of their rice. Others like mixed vegetables or baked bananas. On some of the islands, you might even have fresh eel! The meals you can find in Indonesia are different on each island.

Produce Market In Southern Sulawesi

Pastimes

Sumba Horsemen At Pasola Festival

Indonesians play many common sports, such as soccer and volleyball. They also have a few fun sports of their own. Farmers may hitch two bulls together and race each other. On one island, boys enjoy jumping over a high stone. Some other islanders play a board game with shells or pebbles, called congkak. Whatever the sport, people join in and have fun.

Homemade Game On Sulawesi

SULAWESI

BALI

SUMBA

Young And
Old Play
Soccer
On Bali

SULAWESI

TANA
TORAJA

Wamena

BALI

Muslims Celebrate
Ramadan In
Wamena

Just like many Americans, Indonesians celebrate Christmas and Easter. Many others celebrate a special festival called Ramadan. Even more festivals are held on New Year's Day and on Indonesia's Independence Day— August 17. And each island has its own local festivals too. In Indonesia, there's a party almost every day!

Melasti Ceremony On Bali

Funeral Ceremony In Tana Toraja

With all of its wonderful people, plants, and animals, Indonesia is a very special country. Every year there are more and more people that come to see this different country and its many islands. Perhaps one day you may want to visit the islands of Indonesia, too!

Muslim
Schoolgirl
Of
Sulawesi

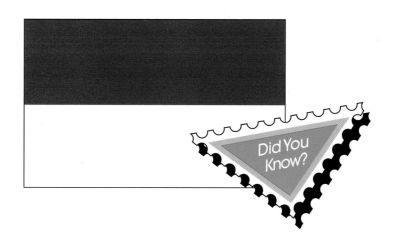

Did You Know?

Indonesia is really called "The Republic of Indonesia." People just say "Indonesia" for short.

Indonesians like to play music on the angklung, an instrument made of bamboo.

Indonesia's roads are always filled with motorbikes. Scooters zip up and down the roads, carrying people and other things.

In the big cities, people use becaks to go places. A becak is a bicycle with a passenger seat.

How Do You Say?

	INDONESIAN	HOW TO SAY IT
Hello	selamat pagi	sch-luh-mut puh-ge
Goodbye	selamat tinggal	sch-luh-mut toen-guhl
Please	silakan	see-luh-kuhn
Thank You	terima kasih	teh-ree-muh kuh-see
One	satu	shu-too
Two	dua	doo-uh
Three	tiga	toe-guh
Indonesia	Indonesia	een-doh-nee-szhuh

capital city (CAP–ih–tuhl SIH–tee)
A capital city is where the government for a country can be found. Indonesia's capital city is Jakarta.

continent (KON–tuh–nent)
Continents are huge areas of land. Most of the continents are separated by oceans.

gong (GONG)
A gong is a flat bell that rings when it is hit with a padded hammer. Some Indonesians use gongs in their music.

tribes (TRYBZ)
Tribes are small groups of people. Many Indonesian tribes have different languages and ways of living.

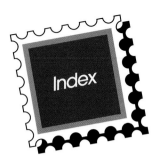